All About Internet FTP

PLUS

Learning and Teaching to Transfer Files on the Internet

Includes Windows and Macintosh diskettes of presentation slides

---

Internet Workshop Series Number 2

Supplement to *Crossing the Internet Threshold*

David F. W. Robison

Library Solutions Press
Berkeley, California

First edition: February 1994
Second printing: August 1994 Minor revisions

Graphics Editors: Catherine Dinnean and Stephanie Lipow

LIBRARY SOLUTIONS PRESS

Sales Office: 1100 Industrial Road, Suite 9
                            San Carlos, CA 94070

Fax orders: 415-594-0411

Telephone orders
and inquiries: 510-841-2636

Editorial Office: 2137 Oregon Street, Berkeley, CA 94705

ISBN: 1-882208-06-4

Table of Contents

Foreword by Anne G. Lipow, Series Coordinator

About This Series...

The volumes of the Internet Workshop Series are the actual workshops, in book form, of expert Internet trainers and include their well-tested lectures, presentation slides (overhead transparencies), exercises, and handouts. The series is, therefore, intended to be useful to two types of reader: the trainer and the learner.

For the trainer, each volume provides a model training tool. With the astounding rate of growth of the Internet, it is likely that as soon you learn about an aspect of the Internet, you'll be asked to explain it to others. Of course, knowing a subject is one thing; teaching it so that your audience learns is quite another. That's the primary reason for this series: by example, to provide the new trainer with the basic skills needed for a successful instructional program. Each volume gives you the words and supporting materials of a proven training session and provides asides to the trainer: for example, advice about how to handle a tricky segment; the principle underlying a particular way of dealing with a topic, the equipment needed for the session. Also, each volumes comes in two editions: the book alone, and the book PLUS. The PLUS editon includes diskettes of the presentation slides, created in PowerPoint, that can be viewed on a Macintosh or DOS-based computer. Trainers are welcome to use all of these materials in conjunction with their own instructional sessions.

For the learner, each volume is a self-paced workshop. The learner is expected to concentrate on the lecture and overheads and to skip the parts addressed to the trainer. However, the lecture and overheads may not be sufficient for understanding the topic because there are two critical pieces of the live workshop that are missing: the online demonstration and the class discussion. To compensate for the absence of online demonstrations, the reader should go through the handouts systematically. And to experience, though in a delayed fashion, the give-and-take between instructor and student, we urge you to note your questions in the margins and email them to the instructors.* Future printings may be revised to answer such questions for later readers.

Whether you are a trainer or a learner, your comments about the usefulness of the volume you are using are most welcome. Please address them to the author.*

---

* Send your comments and questions to the author's email address, which you will find in this section under "About the Author."

. . . and this volume

Just as some people buy for others gifts that really they themselves would like to have, so I chose FTP as a topic to be dealt with early in this series so that I could learn FTP better myself. I have known David Robison and the high quality of his work—both in teaching and writing—for several years. His Internet classes cover a variety of topics, any of which he could well have converted into a printed version. So I was especially pleased when he agreed to this assignment. FTP is difficult to teach, and he does it masterfully, as you will see.

If you are using this book to learn FTP, you'll find the concepts clearly explained, the exercises just what you need to clinch your understanding, and the handouts invaluable for handy reminders later on.

If you are a trainer, you'll find there is built-in flexibility to tailor this workshop to suit your needs. If your schedule permits only a short session, you can go through the lecture (Section B) with highlighter in hand, and highlight the first sentences under each heading to provide you with a well-structured, comprehensive outline to expand in your own words. Or, you can work with some modules and not others, or with just parts of all of them. Or, the full six hours of class, with all the support materials you'll need, is yours for the taking.

About the Author

David F. W. Robison has a Masters Degree in Library and Information Studies from the University of California, Berkeley, and is the founding editor and networking specialist of Current Cites. He is Educational Documentation Specialist at NorthWestNet, a mid-level Internet Service Provider. Formerly, he was Network Resource Coordinator at the Library of the University of California, Berkeley, and taught classes on Internetworking there as well as at the University's Extension program. In 1992 he received the Apple Library of Tomorrow Network Citizen Award for his role in *Current Cites*.

His email address is robison@nwnet.net

A. Preface

Notes on Using This Text

Background Information about FTP

On the Joys of Using and Teaching FTP

Acknowledgements

Preface

Notes on Using This Text

This text serves two purposes: it is a textbook for students of Internet File Transfer Protocol (FTP) as well as a manual for instruction that may be used by teachers of FTP. Section B is a description of FTP, what it is, how it works, and how to make the most use of it. Section C is a set of slides that accompany the descriptive text. They may be photocopied onto transparencies and presented in classes. The exercises in Section D range from beginning to expert. These can be used for self-instruction or in conjunction with classroom instruction. Section D also provides a glossary and cheat sheets or class handouts that are handy guides to FTP to keep right at the computer. Section E offers guidance for teachers of FTP, along with a lesson plan for combining the materials in this text in the classroom situation.

The examples of FTP shown here, and most of the descriptive text, involve the use of FTP on the Unix operating system. This is done for two reasons: first, Unix is the most common operating system used on computers connected to the Internet; and second, Unix FTP employs the most common command-line interface for Internet file transfer.

A note about the fonts used in this book: text that appears in the `courier` font denotes text that is displayed on the computer. **`Courier text`** which appears in **boldface** indicates it should be typed by the user. Text which appears in ***bold italics*** indicates a generic term that the user should replace with a specific term. This includes terms such as file names or user IDs.

For more information about using this book to create a lesson, please refer to "Teaching Tips" in Section E.

In Section B, whenever you see the icon of an overhead transparency projector, that's a signal that there is a corresponding slide in Section C.

Background Information about FTP

Internet File Transfer Protocol (FTP) establishes a specialized interactive online session with a remote computer to allow the transfer of files beween computers on the Internet. FTP is an Internet standard that complies with the Internet protocol suite, Transmission Control Protocol/Internet Protocol (TCP/IP). "FTP" is the name of the Unix program that runs the TCP/IP File Transfer Protocol. Other programs can run the same protocol, and in this book "FTP" will generally refer to any program that can effect this standard form of file transfer. "ftp" in lower case indicates the Unix command which starts the FTP program. FTP can be accomplished through a line-by-line terminal interface, as well as through client software running on a directly connected computer.

FTP permits the transfer of both ASCII text files and binary files (such as programs or compressed files). Files are transferred between two computers that are directly connected to the network (via Ethernet, SLIP/PPP, optical fiber, etc.). It is important to keep in mind exactly where the file is transferred to in relation to your workstation. You may have to download to your desktop computer before you can use the transferred file.

Most files are transferred using "anonymous FTP," where a site administrator has established a portion of the host computer that can be accessed anonymously by any user on the network. Anonymous FTP allows you to connect to a host machine, copy files from that machine to yours, and perhaps copy files to it, all without having an account on that remote machine.

On the Joys of Using and Teaching FTP

FTP gives you the power to transfer large amounts of data on the Internet. This can be both exciting and daunting. It can also lead to the serendipitous discovery of a resource you had no idea existed. During the hands-on section of one class I was teaching, one of the students gave a loud guffaw. I walked over and asked what had happened, whereupon he gleefully replied that he had discovered an archive of the lyrics to Frank Zappa's songs. A happy man he was. It's that kind of experience that makes teaching FTP rewarding for me.

FTP can be complex and sometimes confusing, but it is a subject that should be fun both to teach and learn.

Acknowledgements

I would like to acknowledge Roy Tennant for not only introducing me to the Internet but also encouraging my active involvement in it. Others who have helped, guided, and encouraged my work are: Imani Abalos, Charles Bailey, Alan Emtage, Clifford Lynch, Ann Okerson, Cecilia Preston, Lou Rosenfeld, Craig Summerhill, Ed Vielmetti, and the Electronic Frontier Foundation.

B. The Lecture

The Lecture: All About Internet FTP

A Note to the Instructor

While the class is assembling, display slide 1, the title slide.

Start the class with these important openers:

- *Offer a warm welcome.*

- *Say who you are and talk briefly about your credentials for giving this class.*

- *Review what the class will and will not cover.*

- *If you choose to discuss the "Background Information" presented in the Preface, show slides 3, 4, and 5 here.*

What FTP Can Do and How It Works

Internet File Transfer Protocol, or FTP, enables you to transfer files between a remote computer and yours. FTP sites offer any number of resources for transfer: computer programs (the most typical); full texts of books, journals, and documents of all types; statistical resources; graphical images and sounds. More data is moved around on the network using FTP than any other single operation. Typically forty per cent of the data on the Internet at any one time is file transfer data.

In the briefest terms, FTP is a program on the local machine that makes a connection to a remote machine that also runs an FTP program. The two computers pass commands back and forth and, when instructed by the user (or automated script), send whole files between the two computers. At the end of the session, the user issues a command to quit FTP. Both computers execute the command, and the connection is closed.

By definition, all computers connected to the Internet comply with the Internet standard protocol suite TCP/IP. File transfer is a service of

TCP/IP, using the File Transfer Protocol. At this time, most computers directly connected to the Internet employ the Unix operating system. FTP is also available on numerous operating systems (OS), including:

- DOS
- MS Windows (DOS)
- Macintosh
- X-Windows (Unix)
- NeXTstep

A standard Unix implementation includes the FTP program that runs over TCP/IP. Given the overwhelming majority of users employing the Unix version of FTP on the network, it is understandable that there is some confusion about terminology. Although program names may vary across platforms and from computer to computer, the term "FTP," the verb "to ftp," and the noun "ftp," all refer to the implementation of the File Transfer Protocol running over the TCP/IP protocol suite.

anonymous FTP

 7

Computers connected to the Internet employ security to protect against unauthorized access to non-public files. Depending on the operating system and software, security can protect an entire computer from any unauthorized access (with the exception of possible willful hacking into a system) or protect certain areas or files within a system.

 8

Approximately 1500 computers on the Internet allow unauthenticated users authorized access to public areas of their files. This is known as "anonymous FTP." With anonymous FTP, unauthenticated users can login to a server and perform file exchanges. Anonymous users can transfer (really, copy) files that are on the server and, depending on the permissions established at the host site, also may be able to put files on the server.

 9

An anonymous FTP site is often just a specific area on a computer that also performs other functions (such as email, Gopher, etc.). Anonymous FTP users will generally not have access to all of the files on the host but only to a set of directories specifically set up for anonymous access. Anonymous users connect to the host with the user name anonymous (some machines will also accept guest) which must be lower-case, unabbreviated, and spelled correctly. Often the name of the machine that serves as an FTP site is named *ftp.machinename.location.domain*.

Example: ftp.lib.berkeley.edu

In these cases, the user enters the command:

ftp ftp.*machine.location.domain.*

Many anonymous FTP hosts will request that you input your login or user ID (*e.g.*, *drobison@library.berkeley.edu*) as the password. This information is supposed to be used by administrators to track user patterns, not which files particular users are accessing. Some FTP host programs will check to see that the ID input meets certain basic criteria (such as having the "@" symbol in it), but others will accept anything as the password, including just a carriage return. Since you can not be sure how this login information will be used, you may wish to consider whether or not to enter your real user ID. Some hosts warn users that all transactions are logged, and any user that does not want to have their transactions logged ought to disconnect. Any host can log all transactions along with the user name, but most don't.

Users that have accounts on two Internet-connected host machines can also perform file transfers and may have access to a larger range of files than anonymous users. In this case, you FTP from your initial machine to the remote host and login to your account on that machine, rather than using the anonymous login.

The Simple FTP Interface

The most common, and the original, simple, "vanilla" FTP interface is the Unix command-line interface (also known as the line-by-line terminal interface.) With this method of interaction you start an FTP session with a remote host by invoking the ftp daemon,* or program, on the local machine. The FTP daemon connects to the remote host and from then on, the ftp daemon at the remote site mediates the session.

Only a limited set of commands is available during an FTP session (enough to get the job done!) and each command is visibly accepted and then confirmed by the host machine (see sample session, fig. 1). The messages sent by the remote computer are important to monitor because they inform you about the status of the session. This is especially important when actually transferring files since the FTP daemon will inform you when the transfer connection, itself, is established and how large a file is being transferred. In some instances, the message will also indicate what type of connection is being used for the transfer (ASCII or binary—see below). The host machine will also inform you when the transfer is complete. These status messages are all coded with three digit numbers, but the numbers can be ignored by humans since the text of the message is what is really informative.

* For a definition of "daemon," see the "Glossary" in Section D.

The FTP Session

Executing an FTP session is a simple matter. To start the session, begin at the Unix prompt (usually %) and enter the **ftp** command and the address of the host machine (**ftp *hostname***). Once past the login, you can navigate the directories using the cd command and look at directory listings with the **ls** command (simple listing) or the

dir command (detailed listing including file size). With these commands you can navigate through the directory structure to find a specific file in a known location, or you can explore the archive site and look for files that might be of interest. Once you have identified a file as one you want to transfer, you simply get the file with the **get** command (**get *filename***). Before issuing the **get** command, be

sure you have enough space on your system to store the file; use the **dir** command to check the file size. Text files may be previewed before they are transferred by combining the **get** command with the **more** command in the following way:

> **get *filename* |more.**

The command to get multiple files is **mget** and can be used in conjunction with wildcards (* and ?). See figure 1 for an example of an FTP session.

ASCII vs. Binary Mode

Most FTP daemons are set to ASCII text mode transfer (called "type A") by default. Many file types, however, require the FTP host to be set to perform the transfer in binary mode (called "type I"). It is simple to switch from one to another; the hard part is remembering to do it. Simply enter **binary** to enter binary mode, or **ascii** to return to ASCII mode. If the local host and the remote host are running the same system software (e.g., Unix), binary mode will successfully transfer all file types. See "Downloading" below for more details on file types.

Transferring to a Remote Machine

In the case where you have privileges to transfer (write, or copy) files to a remote machine (either the anonymous FTP host permits this, or you have an account on the remote machine), the command to write files is **put** (**put *filename***). As with **get**, there is a command for writing multiple files to the remote machine; and not surprisingly, it is **mput**.

Long Directory Listings

16

Directory listings can be quite long, and there is no way to stop or slow a listing in progress. While some interfaces (Macintosh, Windows, and X-Windows) will usually allow you to scroll back to view the file listing, you may spend quite a while browsing the list, time that should not be spent still connected to the remote site. A solution is to direct the listing to a file on your local Unix host. This is accomplished from the directory "above" the one you want to list by issuing the command:

> **dir** *local_filename remote_directory*

Then **quit** FTP to free up the port for another user. The file *local_filename* will be in your Unix account in the directory you started from and can be viewed using **more** *local_filename*, or printed to the local printer using **lpr** *local_filename.* If you do not have access to the printer attached to your local Unix host, you will need to print or capture the file using your communications software and the Unix command:

> **cat** *local_filename*

Changing Filenames

Unix filenames have very few restrictions on their format. Although they can not include spaces the way that Macintosh filenames can, they can be quite long, and can include more than one "dot" or period. If you are transferring a file that will be used on a DOS-based computer, you may want to change the name of the file to one with a maximum of eight characters and a file extension with a maximum of three characters during the transfer. This is accomplished by using the following version of the **get** command:

> **get** *remote_filename new_filename*

Changing the filename during transfer is also useful in other situations. Sometimes a file comes with a name that is not helpful to you in your local environment. Changing the filename right away may save you some time and aggravation later on. If you are transferring README files to your local machine, consider changing the name to something more meaningful during the transfer to prevent the situation where you are left with four or five files named with some variation of README. **Caution:** Be sure not to use a filename that is already in your current directory or you will permanently lose the earlier file! See Exercise 3 (Section D) for an example of changing a filename during a file transfer.

When in Limbo...

 17

When you enter the **ftp** command, the local Unix machine starts a program called FTP which initiates a special connection to the remote host. If the connection fails, is suspended in some way, or the host is non-existent or currently unavailable, the local Unix machine may not quit the FTP program. This also occurs when you force the suspension of the connection by issuing the break command, usually <**ctrl-]**> (sometimes designated <**^]**>, where **^** stands for the control key). In this case, you will not be returned to the Unix prompt but the ftp> prompt. At this point the commands available to you change. To close the current connection fully, issue the **close** command. To start another connection issue the **open** command (**open** *hostname*). To close the connection, quit FTP, and return to the Unix prompt, issue the **quit** command.

Figure 1 • **Sample FTP Session**

Connect to FTP server	`library% `**`ftp ftp.cni.org`**
	`Connected to a.cni.org.`
	`220 a.cni.org FTP server (Ultrix Version 4.1 Mon Aug 27`
	`19:11:56 EDT 1990) ready`
	`.`

Login as anonymous (though system knows your user ID)	`Name (ftp.cni.org:drobison): `**`anonymous`** `331 Guest login ok, send ident as password.`
Enter your user ID	`Password:` `230 Guest login ok, access restrictions apply.`

Get directory listing	`ftp> `**`ls`**
	`200 PORT command successful.`
	`150  Opening  data  connection  for  /bin/ls`
	`(128.32.159.12,4041) (0 bytes).`

View directory contents	`.cap`
	`ARL`
	`CNI`
	`bin`
	`current.cites`
	`etc`
	`incoming`
	`members`
	`pub`
	`226 Transfer complete.`
	`65 bytes received in 0.061 seconds (1 Kbytes/s)`

Change to directory "pub"	`ftp> `**`cd pub`** `250 CWD command successful.`

Get directory listing	`ftp> `**`ls`**
	`200 PORT command successful.`
	`150  Opening  data  connection  for  /bin/ls`
	`(128.32.159.12,4042) (0 bytes).`

View directory contents	`FYI-RFC`
	`LITA`
	`MARBI`
	`docs`
	`net-guides`
	`software`
	`226 Transfer complete.`
	`50 bytes received in 0.021 seconds (2.3 Kbytes/s)`

Change to directory "LITA"	`ftp> `**`cd LITA`** `250 CWD command successful.`
Get directory listing	`ftp> `**`ls`** `200 PORT command successful.`

continued on next page

| View directory contents | ```
150  Opening  data  connection  for  /bin/ls
(128.32.159.12,4043) (0 bytes).
.cap
00README
93.ann.neworleans
93.mid.denver
93.new.orleans
contacts
lita-renew
thinking.robots
226 Transfer complete.
105 bytes received in 0.03 seconds (3.4 Kbytes/
    s)
``` |
| Change to directory "thinking.robots" Get directory listing | ```
ftp> cd thinking.robots
250 CWD command successful.
ftp> ls
200 PORT command successful.
150  Opening  data  connection  for  /bin/ls
(128.32.159.12,4044) (0 bytes).
``` |
| View directory contents | ```
Think.Robots.txt
ThinkRobots.sit.hqx
ThinkingRobots.bin
226 Transfer complete.
59 bytes received in 0.02 seconds (2.9 Kbytes/s)
``` |
| Get a copy of file "Think.Robots.txt" | ```
ftp> get Think.Robots.txt
200 PORT command successful.
150 Opening data connection for Think.Robots.txt
    (128.32.159.12,4046) (411443 bytes).
226 Transfer complete.
local: Think.Robots.txt remote: Think.Robots.txt
    419187 bytes received in 67 seconds (6.1
        Kbytes/s)
``` |
| Quit FTP Get local directory listing | ```
ftp> quit
library% ls
``` |
| View local directory contents | ```
Think.Robots.txt   mbox
``` |
| Request a paged display of the file | ```
library% more Think.Robots.txt
THINKING ROBOTS, AN AWARE INTERNET, AND CYBERPUNK
LIBRARIANS

The 1992 LITA President's Program
Presentations by Hans Moravec, Bruce Sterling, and
David Brin
``` |
```

LITA President's Series

R. Bruce Miller and Milton T. Wolf, Editors

Library and Information Technology Association
Chicago, Illinois 1992

This publication is an expanded version of what was distributed at the 1992 American Library Association Annual Conference in San Francisco.
It includes the speakersU presentations and has been reset in easy to read type into a 6-by-9 inch monograph with 200 pages. It will be for sale in mid September 1992 for $22 ($18.70 LITA members, $19.80 ALA members who arenUt LITA members). Order information available from:

Library and Information Technology Association
50 East Huron Street
Chicago IL 60611-2729

Note that in ASCII translation, apostrophes print as "U" as in "speakersU" and "arenUt" in this example.

Downloading

 18

Most people using the Unix command-line FTP program are actually using a desktop personal computer as a terminal to connect to their account on an Internet-connected Unix host. In this case, you FTP the file from the remote host to the Unix machine where your account is (and by default, the file is usually stored in your account). Often, you will need to transfer that file from the Unix machine where your account is to your desktop machine. On your desktop machine, the file can be loaded into your word processing program, graphics program, sound player, or graphics viewer and further manipulated. Or it may be that the file that was transferred was a computer program that you will execute on your desktop computer. Files do not need to be downloaded if they are to be used on the Internet-connected machine itself.

 19

Most files in FTP archives have file extensions that inform you about what type of file it is. The file type will determine whether the file should be transferred in ASCII or binary mode. There may also be a choice of files available. For instance, a single textual document may be available in multiple formats: plain text, PostScript, and WordPerfect. Depending on the software or printer available to you, one of these document types may be the most useful, while the others may be useless. Some file extenstions indicate that the file has been compressed in some way. This means that the file will need to be decompressed before it is used. Some FTP servers perform on-the-fly decompression on demand. Some FTP clients will perform decompression on the local machine (see "FTP Client Software" below). Below is a list of common file extensions, the type of file transfer required, and the software required to use the document (where appropriate). Be aware that a single file may have multiple extensions.

Common File Extensions

Ext.	Type	Explanation
.asc	A	ASCII text document
.exe	B	IBM PC executable
.gif	B	GIF file (use GIF viewer or converter)
.gz	B	GNU Compression (use **gunzip filename** to uncompress) (Unix)
.hqx	A	Encoded with the Macintosh application, BinHex (use BinHex to uncompress)
.mac	B	Macintosh executable
.ps	A	PostScript document
.rtf	A	Rich Text Format (RTF)(use word processor translator)
.sea	B	Self extracting Macintosh archive (double click to uncompress)
.sit	B	Archive created by Macintosh application, StuffIt (use UnstuffIt to uncompress)
.src	B	Source code
.tar	B	Archive created with UNIX tar command (use **tar -xf filename** to uncompress)
.tif	B	TIFF file (a graphics format)
.txt	A	Plain text document
.z	B	GNU Compression (use **gunzip filename** to uncompress) (Unix)
.Z	B	Compressed with UNIX compress command (use **uncompress filename** to uncompress)
.Zip	B	DOS file compressed with PKZIP (use **PKUnzip filename** to decompress)

A = ASCII transfer mode   B = binary transfer mode

Although many applications and compression schemes are associated with a particular operating system, many of these programs are available for other platforms as well (for example, there are both Windows and Macintosh versions of the UNIX Compression scheme). Most compression and decompression programs are available as freeware or shareware on anonymous FTP archives.

Since a single file can have more than one extension, it is important to analyze the file type before transferring it. For example, a file with the double extension .ps.Z is a compressed PostScript file requiring binary transfer, Unix decompression, and PostScript rendering.

20

For use on desktop computers not directly connected to the Internet, with the exception of text-based files, these files must be downloaded to the desktop computer. Downloading is accomplished using a downloading program that is part of the communications software on the desktop personal computer and corresponds to a program on the Unix machine to which the file has been transferred. Popular downloading programs include: Xmodem, Ymodem, Zmodem, and Kermit and most implementations of Unix will have these programs available. Text files may be downloaded using one of these programs, or smaller files may be captured by the communications software as they are displayed on the personal computer's screen by the Unix machine. This is accomplished in just a few easy steps: open a "capture" or "log" file with the communications software, display the text using the Unix **cat** command (**cat filename**) and, once the file has been displayed, close the capture file.

FTP Client Software

 21

FTP client software allows your desktop computer running TCP/IP communications to connect to FTP servers. In the past, available clients were limited to workstations, usally running the Unix operating system. Now, however, client software is being written to run on a number of platforms, allowing desktop computers with full Internet connections (or simulated connections using SLIP, PPP, or ISDN) to make direct FTP connections. There are two distinct advantages to this configuration. First, FTP clients usually employ a better user interface than the standard Unix client. Second, running a client on a desktop computer means that when files are transferred, they are transferred between the remote computer and the computer on your desktop. This obviates the need for an additional step of down- or uploading files. The number and type of clients are growing at a fairly rapid pace. Also, people are writing new clients for various platforms; and the platforms themselves are changing, at times, becoming interchangeable.

Most of these clients are available via anonymous FTP. Below is information you will need to obtain these files, including the Uniform Resource Locators (URLs). The URL is the standard way of identifying files on the Internet. For more information on URLs, see the Glossary in Section D.

When getting these files via anonyous FTP, always read the READMEs for special instructions!

Macintosh Platform

Fetch

Developed at Dartmouth University, Fetch provides an easy and fairly intuitive FTP client for the Macintosh. Fetch opens FTP connections to FTP hosts either on an ad hoc basis or from a predefined profile. With the Fetch client you input the host name or IP address, the user ID (usually **anonymous**), the password, and the initial directory all before the connection is opened. Storing these as predefined profiles or "shortcuts" makes using this client especially easy.

Another advanced feature of the Fetch client is the automated file translation feature. Since many files on FTP servers are coded in a special way (such as with BinHex or StuffIt), either to save space, ease transfer, or both, it is very helpful to have the FTP client perform the translation. While Fetch does not perform all translations (as some of them are proprietary compression schemes), Fetch will read file extensions and offer you a translation choice when a file is selected for transfer. In addition to providing automated file translation for retrieving files, Fetch also provides the same service when loading files onto a server.

One of the nicest features of Fetch is that it is free! Fetch is available from anonymous FTP sites (but, of course, you do need to FTP the program from the archive) and it is also available from other sites that supply shareware and freeware. Fetch is available for anonymous FTP
> at **sumex-aim.stanford.edu**
> in directory **/info-mac/Communication**
> <URL:ftp://sumex-aim.stanford.edu/info-mac/Communication>.

NCSA Telnet

From the National Center for Supercomputing Applications, NCSA Telnet has an FTP program that works much like the Unix FTP client. NCSA Telnet is available for anonymous FTP
> from **ftp.ncsa.uiuc.edu**
> in directory **/Telnet/mac/**
> <URL:ftp://ftp.ncsa.uiuc.edu/Telnet/mac>.

Mosaic for Macintosh

A Macintosh version of the popular Mosaic interface has been released by the National Center for Supercomputing Applications. Mosaic presents a unified graphical user interface for many Internet services, including FTP. Getting a file via anonymous FTP simply requires the user to enter the URL (see below) of the file desired. If the file is a text, it will be retrieved and displayed on the screen. These files, and binary files can also be saved on your local disk. Mac Mosaic is available for anonymous FTP
> from **ftp.ncsa.uiuc.edu**
> in directory **/Mosaic/Mac/**
> <URL:ftp://ftp.ncsa.uiuc.edu/Mosaic/Mac/>.

MS Windows

Rapid Filer

Novell's LAN Workplace for DOS suite of TCP/IP network programs includes a well-designed client called Rapid Filer. Like Fetch (above), Rapid Filer opens FTP connections to FTP hosts either on an *ad hoc* basis, or from a predefined profile. With the Rapid Filer client, you input the host name or IP address, the user ID (usually **anonymous**), the password, and the initial directory, all before the connection is opened. ASCII or binary mode can be selected when defining a profile or left as automatic. In most cases the automatic selection works, but with some systems, binary must be specified manually in Profile Setup.

Unlike Fetch, Rapid Filer sets up a window on the screen with the local file system on the top and the remote file system on the bottom. In addition to a "copy" button that allows you to copy a selected file from one system to another, it is also possible to drag the icon of a file or directory (folder) from one machine to the other. This ability, along with the reasonably powerful file management and directory navigation feature of the program make clear why it is called Rapid Filer. It is also possible to delete files remotely, provided you have such privileges on the remote system.

Mosaic for MS Windows

An MS Windows version of the popular Mosaic interface has been released by the National Center for Supercomputing Applications. Mosaic presents a unified graphical user interface for many Internet services, including FTP. Getting a file via anonymous FTP simply requires the user to enter the URL (see below) of the file desired. If the file is a text or PostScript file, it will be retrieved and displayed on the screen. These files, and binary files can also be saved on your local disk. Mosaic for Windows is available for anonymous FTP

> from **ftp.ncsa.uiuc.edu**
> in directory **/Mosaic/Windows/**
> <URL:ftp://ftp.ncsa.uiuc.edu/Mosaic/Windows>

NCSA Telnet

The National Center for Supercomputing Applications also provides FTP and Telnet services to Internet-connected DOS computers running Windows. NCSA Telnet is available for anonymous FTP

> at **ftp.ncsa.uiuc.edu**
> in directory **/Telnet/windows/**
> <URL:ftp://ftp.ncsa.uiuc.edu/Telnet/windows>

DOS

NCSA Telnet

Also the National Center for Supercomputing Applications provides FTP and Telnet services to Internet-connected DOS computers. The version of FTP that runs with the Telnet client differs little from that with the standard Unix client. NCSA Telnet is available for anonymous FTP

> at **ftp.ncsa.uiuc.edu**
> in directory **/Telnet/msdos/**
> <URL:ftp://ftp.ncsa.uiuc.edu/Telnet/msdos>.

Unix

Mosaic for X-Windows

Mosaic for X-Windows, the first version of the Mosaic (from NCSA) interface, presents a unified graphical user interface for many Internet services, including FTP. Much of the work of FTP is automated in the Mosaic interface. This interface is quickly becoming a standard among users whose equipment can support it. Mosaic is available for anonymous FTP

> from **ftp.ncsa.uiuc.edu**
> in directory **/Mosaic/Mosaic-*** [*i.e.*, various subdirectories]
> <URL:ftp://ftp.ncsa.uiuc.edu/Mosaic/>.

nftp

While technically not a client, nftp can provide some better functionality for Unix hosts running the standard FTP software. Among other things, it allows you to create aliases for ftp sites so that all you need to do is enter **nftp *sitename*** and the program will make the connection using the anonymous login and password. In fact, the sitename can be an abbreviated version of the real sitename. A copy of this program and its manuals is available for anonymous FTP

> at **gauss.technion.ac.il**
> in directory **/nftp/**
> <URL:ftp://gauss.technion.ac.il/nftp/>

Locating Files

22

Locating files on the Internet for any purpose is one of the most difficult aspects of using the net. Most people find out about files that are available from monitoring electronic discussion groups (also called lists or conferences), and electronic and print journals. Locating a known item at a known location on the Internet is easy and a standard Uniform Resource Locator (URL) has been established recently to help provide location information for files of all types (for a description of URLs, see the Glossary, Section D). But when you don't know the location of a file or the location information is incomplete, things can get difficult very quickly. This is not to say that all hope is lost.

There are a number of ways to discover where resources are located, and development work in this area (known as "resource discovery") continues. One organization, the Coalition for Networked Information Discovery and Retrieval (CNIDR – known as "snyder") is a clearinghouse for information on resource discovery tools, user interfaces, and other network services.

The simplest of resource discovery tools is a list of good archive sites with specialties listed. The best of these is *Special Internet Connections*, usually referred to as "Yanoff's List" after its compiler, Scott Yanoff. Copies are available via anonymous ftp from csd4.csd.uwm.edu as file /pub/inet.services.txt <URL:ftp://csd4.csd.edu/pub/inet.services.txt>. Yanoff updates this list on a monthly basis. The list currently contains 27 anonymous FTP sites, organized by subject specialty, along with many Telnet sites. Once at a specific site, it is often fairly easy to find desired materials by browsing through the site.

Browsing Through an Archive Site

23

Many archive sites specialize in certain types of materials; others provide access to an eclectic assortment of materials of many file types. Whether or not the site is dedicated to a particular subject, the resources located there will be organized into different directories by subject. The directory structure is hierarchical with the more general topics at the top of the hierarchy, getting more specific as you move downwards (see fig. 2). This allows for users with little or no previous knowledge of the contents of a site to browse the collection. Most FTP archives put files intended for public use in the pub directory located in the root FTP directory (/pub). There also may be files of interest located in other directories off the root FTP directory; but when in doubt, start in the pub directory.

Some archive sites include indexes (flat text files) and informational files named "README". These files are helpful if you have enough information to search a specific archive or a specific directory at a site, and only when someone has taken the trouble to create such files.

24

Figure 2

Schematic Diagram of UNIX File Organization (Anonymous FTP directory)

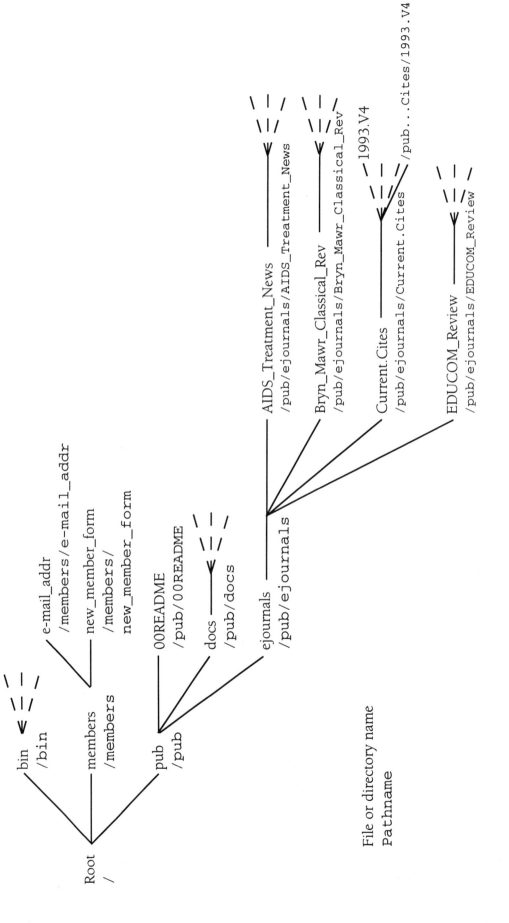

25

Below is a brief list of some interesting FTP sites and their specialties.

Source for:	Site:	IP Address:
Microcomputer software, etc.	wuarchive.wustl.edu	(128.252.135.4)
Macintosh software, etc.	sumex-aim.stanford.edu	(36.44.0.6)
Library-related files	csuvax1.csu.murdoch.edu.au	(134.115.4.1)
	hydra.uwo.ca	(129.100.2.13)
	ftp.unt.edu	(129.120.1.1)
Computers/information	ftp.cni.org	(192.100.21.1)
	ftp.eff.org	(192.88.144.4)
	educom.edu	(192.52.179.128)
Center for Text & Tech.	ftp.guvax.georgetown.edu	(141.161.1.2)
Supreme Court Rulings	ftp.cwru.edu	(192.22.4.2)
Medical materials	ftp.sura.net	(128.167.254.179)
List of discussion lists	ftp.nisc.sri.com	(192.33.33.22)
Online Book Initiative (/obi)	ftp.std.com	(192.74.137.7)

Another way to browse both archive directories and archives themselves is via a Gopher. Some Gopher servers offer listings of FTP archives and their contents. To actually transfer files such as graphics and sounds using the current version of Gopher, you will need a Gopher client. However, when you have little idea of which archive to search, a larger index is necessary. This is where the archie service is so valuable. Archie is, by far, the most popular and replete source of information about files available for FTP.

archie

26

The archie service—short for "archive" (not a reference to the comic book character)—is a set of mirrored, automatically updated, and keyword searchable indexes of most of the anonymous FTP archive sites in the world. Archie was developed by Alan Emtage, Bill Heelan, and Peter Deutsch as an in-house time-saving system for students, faculty, and staff at McGill University for locating FTP'able programs on the Internet. Once the index was made publicly available on the Internet through Telnet (remote login), the use of the database skyrocketed. Usage of the original system grew so much that at one point half of all Canadian network traffic was archie traffic. This incoming traffic so clogged the Canadian network that it was virtually impossible for McGill users to travel the Internet beyond their campus. Not surprisingly, McGill's administrators required the archie developers to make some changes. The result was that the service was installed at a number of different sites. At this time there are 14 mirrored sites around the world.

archie Sites

Each archie site is updated automatically every month by the archie indexing program on a rotating basis. This means that any site will be no more than one month out of date. The archie program indexes only sites that site administrators have indicated may be indexed. Some administrators do not allow indexing because they do not want the publicity generated by it. Although archie was designed to assist users in locating programs available for FTP, archie actually indexes all files at the designated sites. The origins of archie are still evident, however, in the primary search command: **prog** (which stands for "program"). Archie client software is available for anonymous FTP at each archie server site. It is strongly recommended that Internet-connected machines install and use clients to speed searches and reduce overall load on the servers.

As of this writing, the following servers are available. It is prudent to connect to the site closest to you to reduce load across the network. On the other hand, at prime time in your location (6:00 a.m. – 7:00 p.m.), an archie site at a distant location may have fewer users connected.

archie.rutgers.edu	128.6.18.15	(Rutgers University)
archie.unl.edu	129.93.1.14	(University of Nebraska in Lincoln)
archie.ans.net	147.225.1.10	(ANS archie server)
archie.au	139.130.4.6	(Australian server)
archie.funet.fi	128.214.6.100	(European server in Finland)
archie.doc.ic.ac.uk	146.169.11.3	(European server in the UK)
archie.ac.il	132.65.20.254	(Israeli server)
archie.wide.ad.jp	133.4.3.6	(Japanese server)
archie.ncu.edu.tw	140.115.19.24	(Taiwanese server)
archie.sogang.ac.kr	163.239.1.11	(Korean server)
archie.nz	130.195.9.4	(New Zealand server)
archie.kuis.kyoto-u.ac.jp	130.54.20.1	(Japanese server)
archie.th-darmstadt.de	130.83.128.111	(German server)
archie.luth.se	130.240.18.4	(Swedish server)

The archie Session

Archie can be used with little knowledge of how it works or of the advanced commands. Archie indexes the directories and file names of the archive sites. Since the directory and subdirectory names have some meaning regarding their contents, they can be used for the keywords in the search statement.

 27

Archie has four search modes, which affect the way the search term is matched to entries in the index. With **exact** searching (**set search exact**), archie will match upper and lower case and use no truncation on the search term. With this type of search, archie treats the "/" as the word delimiter. A less exact search is the **subcase** search (**set search subcase**). Here, archie remains case sensitive, but will include automatic right and left truncation. Another type of search is the **sub** search (**set search sub**). This is the broadest archie search, where matches are case insensitive, and include both right and left truncation. The last search mode is the **regex**, or regular expression, search (**set search regex**), where the user has full control over the use of truncation and wildcards. For a more detailed explanation of regex searching, enter **help *regex*** while in archie.

The following examples illustrate the different results retrieved by the **exact**, **subcase**, and **sub** search modes:

exact search	archie> prog grass
would find	/pub/poetry/whitman/grass
but not	/pub/poetry/whitman/leaves.of.grass
or	/pub/poetry/whitman/grass.txt
or	/pub/poetry/Whitman/Grass

subcase search	archie> prog grass
would find	/pub/poetry/whitman/grass
	/pub/poetry/whitman/leaves.of.grass
and	/pub/poetry/whitman/grass.txt
but not	/pub/poetry/Whitman/Grass

sub search	archie> prog grass
would find	/pub/poetry/whitman/grass
	/pub/poetry/whitman/leaves.of.grass
	/pub/poetry/whitman/grass.txt
and	/pub/poetry/Whitman/Grass

During searches, archie displays the number of hits and the percentage of the database searched. You can monitor the search and break it, if the number of hits begins to get too large, by using `<ctrl-c>` or `<^c>`. Once the search is ended, either because the entire database has been searched or you have stopped the search, archie displays the results automatically. Archie can also be instructed to mail the results to the user (`mail mensch@library.metro.org`).

archie's `whatis`

Archie has another feature called "whatis". With this command and a keyword (`whatis keyword`), you can search the software description database. Not all of the software indexed by archie has a description, but this database is still quite useful. This is helpful when you are looking for a program to perform a certain function, but do not know the name of any packages that perform it. Once archie lists the name(s) of the program(s), you can search the regular archie database using `prog` for the location of the program.

archie Results

Archie results must be analyzed by the user. Information about a file is spread out across the entire pathname of the file. The archie index only includes the part of the pathname as far as it matches the search (reading the pathname left to right). This means that archie may not lead you to an exact file name, but it will point you in a likely direction for finding a file.

Additional help using archie may be obtained by entering the `help` command in archie.

Keeping Current

As with other areas of networking, one of the best ways to stay current is to join an electronic discussion in the subject area of interest. Subscribers to electronic discussions frequently post information on the availability of resources through anonymous FTP. There are also some general interest lists that announce new network resources, FTP as well as other types of resources. One such list is the Net-Resources list

`(net-resources@is.internic.net)`.

To subscribe to this list, send the following message to

`listserv@is.internic.net:`

`subscribe net-resources` *your name*

and substitute your own name for *your name.*

There is another list available from the same listserver called Net-Happenings which distributes information on network tools, conferences, calls for papers, news items, new mailing lists, electronic newsletters, and more. To subscribe to it, simply follow the directions above but change the name of the list to "net-happenings". The Net-Resources list distributes eight to ten messages per week, while Net-Happenings distributes five to eight messages per day. Some users subscribe to both lists. Of course, both print and electronic journals are useful in identifying new resources, as are personal contacts (either in-person or virtual).

Summary

 28

Note to instructor:

To close the session, highlight the major ideas you want your audience to remember.

C. Presentation Slides

1.   Title slide
2.   Outline
3.   Basic Concepts
4.   What FTP Does (Part 1)
5.   What FTP Does (Part 2)
6.   How FTP Works
7.   File Security
8.   anonymous FTP (General)
9.   anonymous FTP: How to Start A Session
10.   The Simple FTP Interface
11.   The FTP Session (Steps 1–3)
12.   The FTP Session (Steps 4–6)
13.   Other FTP Commands
14.   ASCII vrs, Binary Mode
15.   Transferring Files to a Remote Machine
16.   Problem: Long Directory Listings
17.   To End A Session
18.   Downloading:
       If your Workstation is a Terminal
19.   Downloading: File Extensions
20.   Two Ways to Download
21.   FTP Client Software
22.   Locating Files
23.   Browsing an Archive Site
24.   Directory Structure
25.   Sample FTP Sites
26.   archie
27.   archie's Four Search Modes
28.   Summary

All About Internet FTP

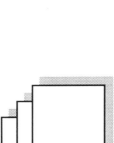

Outline

- ◆ Introduction
- ◆ How FTP Works
- ◆ Anonymous FTP
- ◆ FTP Session
- ◆ Downloading
- ◆ FTP Client Software
- ◆ Locating Files

Basic Concepts

- **TCP/IP**
  - ✓ The set (suite) of protocols, or rules, governing the transfer of all data on the Internet
  - ✓ FTP is one of the TCP/IP protocols

- **FTP is a Unix program governing the transfer of files**

- **FTP is an interactive session between two computers**

- **ftp (lower case) is a Unix command**

What FTP Does

Transfers remote files to your computer

- **File format**
  - ✓ ASCII text files
  - ✓ binary text files
- **File contents**
  - ✓ full text
  - ✓ computer programs
  - ✓ statistical resources
  - ✓ graphical images
  - ✓ sounds

What FTP Does

- Computers must be directly connected to the Internet via:
  - ✓ Ethernet
  - ✓ SLIP/PPP
  - ✓ Optical fiber

- If your workstation is not directly connected, download from your host computer to your desktop to manipulate file

How FTP Works

Internet Operating Systems

- Unix is most commonly used

- FTP is standard on Unix Internet connections

- FTP also available on other operating systems

  - ⌄ DOS
  - ⌄ Windows (DOS)
  - ⌄ Macintosh
  - ⌄ NeXt

anonymous FTP

File Security

- Internet security protects against unauthorized access to non-public files

- Some computers protect only certain areas or files

- Unprotected areas contain files accessible via "anonymous FTP"

anonymous FTP

- ◆ Allows unauthenticated users access to public areas
  - √ No need to have an account on remote computer
  - √ No need for private password

- ◆ Any Internet user can login to a server and perform file exchanges
  - √ Transfer (copy) file from server
  - √ Put files onto server (maybe)

- ◆ Limited access
  - √ Usually access is only to files within a specific set of directories, not to all files on host

anonymous FTP

How to Start a Session

1. Connect to host:

   `ftp hostname`

2. Login with user name: `anonymous`

   ✓ lower case

   ✓ unabbreviated

   ✓ spelled correctly

3. For password, enter your user ID

   Example: `mensch@library.metro.com`

The Simple FTP Interface

- Unix command-line interface
  - √ Most common interface; "vanilla"
  - √ Line-by-line terminal interface
- How it works
  - √ User invokes ftp "daemon" program on local machine
  - √ ftp daemon connects to remote host
  - √ ftp daemon at remote site mediates session
  - √ very informative messages, including status of session, when transfer is complete

The FTP Session: 6 steps

1. At UNIX Prompt (usually %)

   enter ftp command and host machine address

   Example: `% ftp ftp.cni.org`

2. Login

   At name: type   `anonymous`

   At password: type `your@user.id`

   (prompt changes to   `ftp>`)

3. Search directories for file

   Type `cd` *directory name*

   `cd` = change directory

   Example: `cd pub`

The FTP session (cont'd)

4. List files in directory

   Type `ls`   (simple listing)

   or   `dir`   (gives details, incl. file size)

5. Find specific file in known directory

   or

   Explore site for offerings of interest

6. To transfer a file

   type `get filename`

   Example: `get Think.Robots.txt`

Other FTP Commands

◆ **To preview file before you transfer**

get filename |more

◆ **To get multiple files**

mget

Combine file names with wildcards (* and ?)

ASCII vs. Binary Mode

- ASCII
  - ✓ common default text transfer mode
  - ✓ called "type A" transfer mode
- Binary
  - ✓ many types of files require transfer in binary mode
  - ✓ called "type I" transfer mode
- To switch
  - ✓ type binary to enter binary mode
  - ✓ type ascii to return to ASCII mode

Transferring Files
to a Remote Machine

- ◆ You can "write" files to a remote machine when:

  √ the Anonymous FTP host permits it

  √ you have an account on that machine

- ◆ Commands

  √ put (put *filename*) to transfer a single file

  √ mput to transfer multiple files

  Combine file names with wildcards (* and ?)

The FTP Session

Problem: Long Directory Listings

◆ To browse, create local file

  ✓ speeds your browsing time

  ✓ reduces time connected to remote host

◆ The steps

  ✓ Move to directory "above" directory you want to list

  ✓ Enter `dir` *remote_directory local_filename*

  ✓ Changing the file name during transfer:

    `get` *remote_filename new_filename*

The FTP Session

To End a Session

- **At FTP prompt (ftp>)**
  - √ close   to close current connection fully
  - √ open   to start another connection
    (open hostname)
  - √ quit   to quit FTP and return to UNIX
    prompt

- **When in limbo...**
  - √ Symptom: you want to quit FTP but your local machine won't
  - √ Solution: issue escape command
    ctrl-]   or ^]

Downloading

If your workstation is a terminal. . .

◆ File is FTP'd from remote host to Unix machine where your account is

◆ File is stored where your account is

◆ Download to your desktop computer if you want to use file with your

   ✓ word processing program

   ✓ graphics program

   ✓ sound player

   ✓ or if file is a program itself

◆ No need to download if file will be used on your local host machine

Downloading: file extensions

- They tell:
  - type of file
  - whether to download in ASCII or Binary
  - whether compressed
    (must be decompressed before use)

- Some text files in multiple formats
  - plain text
  - PostScript
  - word processing

Two Ways to Download

♦ Use program on your host machine that corresponds to program on your desktop's communications software

    Examples: Xmodem   Zmodem

                    Ymodem   Kermit

♦ For smaller text files, use desktop communications software to capture (log) screens

    ✓ Open "capture" or "log" file on your desktop

    ✓ Display text using Unix cat comand

        `cat filename`

    ✓ When display is complete, close capture file

FTP Client Software

- Allows desktop computer with full Internet connection to make direct FTP connection

- Provides friendlier user interface

- Transfers files directly to your desktop (eliminates downloading step)

Locating Files

- ◆ Location information = site and file name

- ◆ If information incomplete, use
  - √ archive site directories
  - √ resources subject listings
  - √ Gopher
  - √ archie

- ◆ Resource discovery tools
  - √ CNIDR ("snyder") clearinghouse
  - √ Lists of archive sites by specialities
    (e.g., Yanoff)
  - √ Uniform Resource Locators (URLs)

Locating Files:
Browsing an archive site

- ◆ Directories are organized by subject

- ◆ Directory structure: hierarchical
  - ✓ General topics at top
  - ✓ More specific as you move downwards

- ◆ Public files usually in "pub" directory
  located in root FTP directory (/pub)

Directory Structure

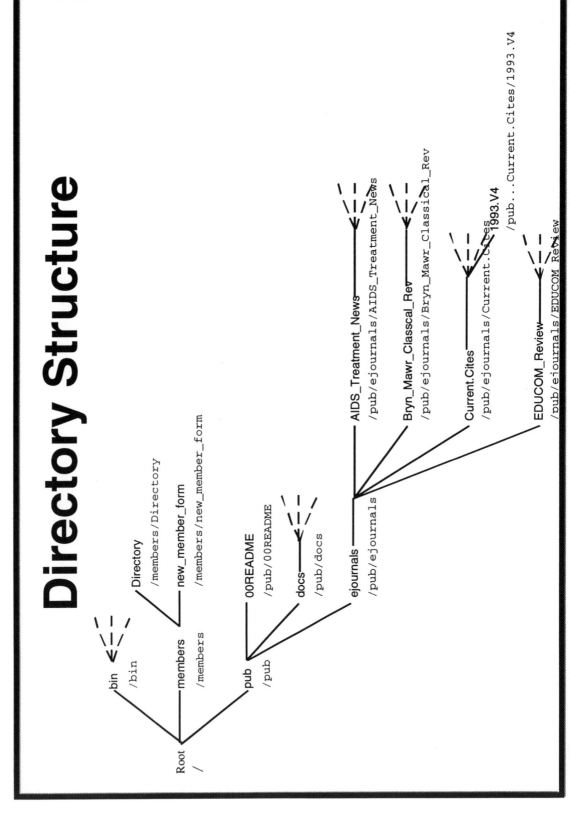

Sample FTP Sites

Source for:	Site:	IP Address:
Microcomputer software, etc.	wuarchive.wustl.edu	(128.252.135.4)
Macintosh software, etc.	sumex-aim.stanford.edu	(36.44.0.6)
Library-related files	csuvax1.csu.murdoch.edu.au	(134.115.4.1)
	hydra.uwo.ca	(129.100.2.13)
Computers/information	ftp.cni.org	(192.100.21.1)
	ftp.eff.org	(192.88.144.4)
	educom.edu	(192.52.179.128)
Supreme Court Rulings	ftp.cwru.edu	(192.22.4.2)
Medical materials	ftp.sura.net	(128.167.254.179)
List of discussion lists	ftp.nisc.sri.com	(192.33.33.22)
Online Book Initiative (/obi)	ftp.std.com	(192.74.137.7)

Locating Files: archie

- Indexes nearly all anonymous FTP servers
- Available at several sites
- Is automatically updated
- Searches your pattern in pathname
  - ✓ Search statement: prog word/pattern
  - ✓ archie displays results
  - ✓ Will email results with "mail" command
    example: mail mensch@library.metro.org

archie's Four Search Modes

- exact — searches for exact match
- subcase — right and left truncation
- sub — ignores upper/lower case, and includes R & L truncation
- regex — = "regular expression" User controls truncation and wildcards

Summary

- FTP is a service of TCP/IP

- Over 1500 anonymous FTP sites

- FTP transfers files between Internet-connected computers

- Downloading to desktop computer sometimes necessary

- Locating files simplified by archie

D. Supporting Materials

Glossary

Exercises

- Getting a Simple Text File

- Reading a Text File without Transferring It

- Changing Local File Names and Directories

- Getting a Program (DOS)

- Getting a Font (Macintosh)

- Locating and Getting a Graphics Files

Handouts

Glossary

archie

A contraction of the word "archive," archie is an online index of over 1500 anonymous FTP archives. Archie is available from a number of mirrored Internet sites around the globe. These sites are automatically updated on a monthly basis. Archie is available via Telnet or through client access.

The Clearinghouse for Networked Information Discovery and Retrieval (CNIDR)

CNIDR is an NSF-funded organization created to act as an information clearinghouse for network discovery and retrieval tools. CNIDR also participates in the ongoing development of some of these tools. More information about CNIDR and its resources (including clients available for downloading) is accessible on both and FTP and Gopher server: <URL:ftp://ftp.cnidr.org/> and <URL:gopher://gopher.cnidr.org:70>.

Daemon

A Unix daemon (pronounced "demon") is the central consituent program that performs a specific operation. The deamon can operate in the background without the user monitoring or guiding its operation (within certain parameters). In the case of FTP, the user command **ftp** starts the ftp daemon which, in turn, makes the connection to the remote computer and negotiates the session.

FAQs (Frequently Asked Questions)

FAQs (pronounced "fax") are lists of frequently asked questions about specific topics (and their answers!) provided by network users to help neophytes. FAQs can be found in many locations and through multiple modes of access (FTP, Gopher, Usenet, LISTSERVs, etc.). Keep an eye out for these, even if you are not a neophyte, they're sure to help.

IP Address (see also: Transmission Control Protocol/ Internet Protocol (TCP/IP))

The IP address of an Internet node or computer is the numeric address associated with the network interface in the computer. While humans typically use human language addresses to describe computers, the Internet uses the numeric IP address. The IP address is made up of four 8-bit (with values from 0-255) numbers separated by decimals (e.g., 132.24.210.4). The first two sections indicate the location, the third indicates the local subnet, while the last indicates the specific computer, or if the last block is just a zero, it is a router.

Telnet

Telnet is a service of TCP/IP that allows one computer connected to the Internet to establish an interactive session with another Internet-connected computer. When this type of connection is established, you can to use the remote computer as if it were on your own desktop.

Transmission Control Protocol/Internet Protocol (TCP/IP)

TCP/IP (as it is known), is the suite of protocols that governs communications on the Internet. In fact, any computer network connected to the Internet that supports TCP/IP becomes a part of the Internet (assuming two-way communication is permitted). TCP controls the flow of data over the network, while IP controls how data packets are properly routed through the addressing system.

Uniform Resource Locator

A recent development on the Internet is the Uniform Resource Locator (URL). Though there is still some discussion on its final form, the URL is an international standard for describing the location of an instance of a file. The URL is analogous to a call number and is a concatenation of the scheme of a resource (FTP, Gopher, Telnet, etc.) and the full pathname of the resource. Also under development are Uniform Resource Numbers, analogous to ISBNs and ISSNs, which will be mapped to the URLs of all registered locations of each file through centralized registrars. URLs and URNs are examples of Uniform Resource Identifiers (URIs). The advantage of URLs is that they are easily constructed and transcribable by both computers and people. For instance, the URL for one instance of the document describing URLs is
<URL:ftp://ns.ripe.net/draft-ietf-uri-url-01.txt>
indicating the availability of the file via FTP at the location ns.ripe.net, with the pathname draft-ietf-uri-url-01.txt.
A PostScript® version is also available at that location
<URL:ftp://ns.ripe.net/draft-ietf-uri-url-01.ps>
URLs need not be preceded by the designation "URL:" or it may be written as "url:".

Wide-Area Information Server (WAIS)

The Wide-Area Information Server is an index service for full-text files at multiple, distributed sites. WAIS allows you to search multiple databases and receive a ranked list of the aggregated results. WAIS is available via Telnet, or through a local client.

World-Wide Web (WWW or W³)

The World-Wide Web is a hypertext knowledge system developed at CERN to organize data for researchers. The system allows you to traverse the web of knowledge through the use of hypertext links. WWW is available via Telnet or through a local client.

Exercise 1: Level 1

Getting a Simple Text File

Connect to ftp.cni.org (The Coalition for Networked Information)

```
% ftp ftp.cni.org
```

Login as anonymous; password is your email address

```
Name: anonymous
Password: username@machine.location.domain
```

Change working directory to pub

```
ftp> cd pub
```

Change working directory to LITA

```
ftp> cd LITA
```

Get README file

```
ftp> get README
```

Quit FTP

```
ftp> quit
```

View the file using the Unix more command

```
% more README
```

Exercise: Level 2

Reading a Text File Without Transferring It

Connect to `ftp.cni.org` (The Coalition for Networked Information)

% **ftp ftp.cni.org**

Login as anonymous; password is your email address

Name: **anonymous**

Password: **username@machine.location.domain**

Change working directory to pub

ftp> **cd pub**

Change working directory to LITA

ftp> **cd LITA**

Change working directory to `thinking.robots`

ftp> **cd thinking.robots**

Read Think.Robots by piping the get command through the more command

ftp> **get Think.Robots |more**

When done reading, type q or quit to stop the display

Quit FTP

ftp> **quit**

Exercise: Level 3

Changing Local File Names and Directories

Create a local directory called `etexts` (for electronic texts)

`% `**`mkdir etexts`**

Connect to std.world.com (home of the Online Book Initiative)

`% `**`ftp ftp.std.com`**

Login as anonymous; password is your email address

`Name: `**`anonymous`**

`Password: `**`username@machine.location.domain`**

Change working directory to obi/`Martin.Luther.King`

`ftp> `**`cd obi/Martin.Luther.King`**

Change the local directory to `etexts`

`ftp> `**`lcd etexts`**

Get `free.at.last` and change the name to `MLKs_dream`

`ftp> `**`get free.at.last MLKs_dream`**

Quit FTP

`ftp> `**`quit`**

To read the text, use the `more` command

`% `**`more MLKs_dream`**

To quit reading before the end of the document is reached, type q

The file is currently located in your account on your Internet-connected host computer. If this host is not a computer on your desktop, you may want to download or capture this file onto your desktop computer. With a short text file such as this, it is easiest to use your communications software's screen capture or log function. Simply turn on the screen capture or log function and create a file name for the incoming file on your local disk, then issue the Unix command to display the text of the file:

`% `**`cat MLKs_dream`**

Exercise: Level 4 (DOS)

Getting a Program — PKZIP

Connect to `nic.cerf.net` (the CERFNet Network Information Center)

`% `**`ftp nic.cerf.net`**

Login as anonymous; password is your email address

Name: **anonymous**

Password: ***username@machine.location.domain***

Change working directory to `pub/infomagic_cd/dos/tools`

`ftp> `**`cd pub/infomagic_cd/dos/tools`**

Change the transfer mode to `binary`

`ftp> `**`binary`**

Get the file `pkzip.exe`

`ftp> `**`get pkzip.exe`**

Quit FTP once the transfer is complete

`ftp> `**`quit`**

If this transfer was performed using a dial-up or terminal connection to a Unix host, the file will need to be downloaded to the desktop DOS machine to be used. Perform the transfer using the communications software on your desktop computer. Once the file has been downloaded to the desktop computer it can be run as an executable file.

Exercise: Level 4 (Macintosh)

Getting a Font

Connect to sumex-aim.stanford.edu (the Macintosh archive at Stanford University, considered the best)

```
% ftp sumex-aim.stanford.edu
```

Login as anonymous; password is your email address

```
Name: anonymous
Password: username@machine.location.domain
```

Change working directory to info-mac

```
ftp> cd info-mac
```

Change working directory to font

```
ftp> cd font
```

Get the Cyrillic font using the get command

```
ftp> get cyrillic-misc.hqx
```

When the transfer is complete, quit FTP

```
ftp> quit
```

If this transfer was performed using a dial-up or terminal connection to a Unix host, the file will need to be downloaded to the desktop Macintosh to be used. Perform the transfer using the communications software on your desktop computer. Once the font has been downloaded to the desktop computer it can be placed in the fonts folder, system folder, or loaded with the Font/DA Mover, depending on the Macintosh system you are running.

Exercise: Level 5 (Graphics)

Locating and Then Getting a GIF File

Telnet to archie
```
% telnet archie.unl.edu  (or other archie site)
```
Login as archie
```
login: archie
```
Set the terminal type
Search on the keyword quake
```
archie> prog quake
```
Wait for the search to end; archie displays the hits

Scroll back to locate the subdirectory quake_gif and note the full pathname and host listed; if you do not have a scroll feature on your computer, have archie send you the file via email by typing **mail** and then *your email address*, then <return>.

Quit archie
```
archie> quit
```
Connect to the FTP server that has the file you want
```
% ftp dix.gps.caltech.edu
```
Login as anonymous; password is your email address
```
Name: anonymous
Password: username@machine.location.domain
```
Change the working directory to pub/outgoing/quake_gif
```
ftp> cd pub/outgoing/quake_gif
```
Change the transfer mode to binary
```
ftp> binary
```
Get one of the files using the get command
```
ftp> get filename.gif
```
When the transfer is complete, quit FTP
```
ftp> quit
```

If this transfer was performed using a dial-up or terminal connection to a Unix host, the file will need to be downloaded to the desktop machine to be used. Perform the transfer using the communications software on your desktop computer, then use a GIF viewer on your desktop computer to view the picture you have just retrieved.

Handouts

Presentation Slides (mini-size)

Internet File Transfer Protocol

FTP Commands

archie: The Index of FTP Archives

PRESENTATION SLIDES

All About Internet FTP

Outline

- ◆ Introduction
- ◆ How FTP Works
- ◆ Anonymous FTP
- ◆ FTP Session
- ◆ Downloading
- ◆ FTP Client Software
- ◆ Locating Files

Basic Concepts

- ◆ TCP/IP
  - ✓ The set (suite) of protocols, or rules, governing the transfer of all data on the Internet
  - ✓ FTP is one of the TCP/IP protocols
- ◆ FTP is a Unix program governing the transfer of files
- ◆ FTP is an interactive session between two computers
- ◆ ftp (lower case) is a Unix command

What FTP Does

Transfers remote files to your computer

- ◆ File format
  - ✓ ASCII text files
  - ✓ binary text files
- ◆ File contents
  - ✓ full text
  - ✓ computer programs
  - ✓ statistical resources
  - ✓ graphical images
  - ✓ sounds

What FTP Does

- ◆ Computers must be directly connected to the Internet via:
  - ✓ Ethernet
  - ✓ SLIP/PPP
  - ✓ Optical fiber

- ◆ If your workstation is not directly connected, download from your host computer to your desktop to manipulate file

How FTP Works

Internet Operating Systems

- ◆ Unix is most commonly used
- ◆ FTP is standard on Unix Internet connections
- ◆ FTP also available on other operating systems
  - ✓ DOS
  - ✓ Windows (DOS)
  - ✓ Macintosh
  - ✓ NeXt

anonymous FTP

File Security

◆ Internet security protects against unauthorized access to non-public files

◆ Some computers protect only certain areas or files

◆ Unprotected areas contain files accessible via "anonymous FTP"

anonymous FTP

◆ Allows unauthenticated users access to public areas
  ✓ No need to have an account on remote computer
  ✓ No need for private password
◆ Any Internet user can login to a server and perform file exchanges
  ✓ Transfer (copy) file from server
  ✓ Put files onto server (maybe)
◆ Limited access
  ✓ Usually access is only to files within a specific set of directories, not to all files on host

anonymous FTP

How to Start a Session
1. Connect to host:
   ftp *hostname*
2. Login with user name: anonymous
   ✓ lower case
   ✓ unabbreviated
   ✓ spelled correctly
3. For password, enter your user ID
   Example: mensch@library.metro.com

The Simple FTP Interface

◆ Unix command-line interface
  ✓ Most common interface; "vanilla"
  ✓ Line-by-line terminal interface
◆ How it works
  ✓ User invokes ftp "daemon" program on local machine
  ✓ ftp daemon connects to remote host
  ✓ ftp daemon at remote site mediates session
  ✓ very informative messages, including status of session, when transfer is complete

The FTP Session: 6 steps

1. At UNIX Prompt (usually %)
   enter ftp command and host machine address
   Example: % ftp ftp.cni.org
2. Login
   At name: type anonymous
   At password: type your@user.id
   (prompt changes to ftp>)
3. Search directories for file
   Type cd *directory name*
   cd = change directory
   Example: cd pub

The FTP session (cont'd)

4. List files in directory
   Type ls (simple listing)
   or dir (gives details, incl. file size)

5. Find specific file in known directory
   or
   Explore site for offerings of interest

6. To transfer a file
   type get *filename*
   Example: get Think.Robots.txt

Other FTP Commands

- To preview file before you transfer
  get filename |more

- To get multiple files
  mget
  Combine file names with wildcards (* and ?)

ASCII vs. Binary Mode

- ASCII
  - ✓ common default text transfer mode
  - ✓ called "type A" transfer mode
- Binary
  - ✓ many types of files require transfer in binary mode
  - ✓ called "type I" transfer mode
- To switch
  - ✓ type binary to enter binary mode
  - ✓ type ascii to return to ASCII mode

Transferring Files to a Remote Machine

- You can "write" files to a remote machine when:
  - ✓ the Anonymous FTP host permits it
  - ✓ you have an account on that machine

- Commands
  - ✓ put (put *filename*) to transfer a single file
  - ✓ mput to transfer multiple files
    Combine file names with wildcards (* and ?)

The FTP Session

Problem: Long Directory Listings
- To browse, create local file
  - ✓ speeds your browsing time
  - ✓ reduces time connected to remote host
- The steps
  - ✓ Move to directory "above" directory you want to list
  - ✓ Enter dir *remote_directory local_filename*
  - ✓ Changing the file name during transfer:
    get *remote_filename new_filename*

The FTP Session

To End a Session
- At FTP prompt (ftp>)
  - ✓ close to close current connection fully
  - ✓ open to start another connection
    (open hostname)
  - ✓ quit to quit FTP and return to UNIX prompt
- When in limbo...
  - ✓ Symptom: you want to quit FTP but your local machine won't
  - ✓ Solution: issue escape command
    ctrl-] or ^]

Downloading

If your workstation is a terminal. . .
- File is FTP'd from remote host to Unix machine where your account is
- File is stored where your account is
- Download to your desktop computer if you want to use file with your
  - ✓ word processing program
  - ✓ graphics program
  - ✓ sound player
  - ✓ or if file is a program itself
- No need to download if file will be used on your local host machine

Downloading: file extensions

- ◆ They tell:
    - ✓ type of file
    - ✓ whether to download in ASCII or Binary
    - ✓ whether compressed
       (must be decompressed before use)

- ◆ Some text files in multiple formats
    - ✓ plain text
    - ✓ PostScript
    - ✓ word processing

Two Ways to Download

- ◆ Use program on your host machine that corresponds to program on your desktop's communications software
    - Examples: Xmodem   Zmodem
                 Ymodem   Kermit
- ◆ For smaller text files, use desktop communications software to capture (log) screens
    - ✓ Open "capture" or "log" file on your desktop
    - ✓ Display text using Unix cat comand
       `cat filename`
    - ✓ When display is complete, close capture file

FTP Client Software

- ◆ Allows desktop computer with full Internet connection to make direct FTP connection

- ◆ Provides friendlier user interface

- ◆ Transfers files directly to your desktop (eliminates downloading step)

Locating Files

- ◆ Location information = site and file name
- ◆ If information incomplete, use
    - ✓ archive site directories
    - ✓ resources subject listings
    - ✓ Gopher
    - ✓ archie
- ◆ Resource discovery tools
    - ✓ CNIDR ("snyder") clearinghouse
    - ✓ Lists of archive sites by specialties
       (e.g., Yanoff)
    - ✓ Uniform Resource Locators (URLs)

Locating Files: Browsing an archive site

- ◆ Directories are organized by subject

- ◆ Directory structure: hierarchical
    - ✓ General topics at top
    - ✓ More specific as you move downwards

- ◆ Public files usually in "pub" directory located in root FTP directory (/pub)

Directory Structure

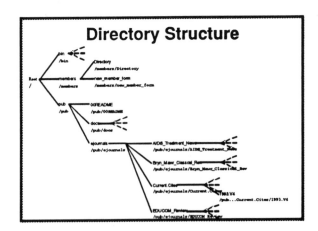

Sample FTP Sites

Source for:	Site:	IP Address:
Microcomputer software, etc.	wuarchive.wustl.edu	(128.252.135.4)
Macintosh software, etc.	sumex-aim.stanford.edu	(36.44.0.6)
Library-related files	csuvax1.csu.murdoch.edu.au	(134.115.4.1)
	hydra.uwo.ca	(129.100.2.13)
Computers/Information	ftp.cni.org	(192.100.21.1)
	ftp.eff.org	(192.88.144.4)
	educom.edu	(192.52.179.128)
Supreme Court Rulings	ftp.cwru.edu	(192.22.4.2)
Medical materials	ftp.sura.net	(128.167.254.179)
List of discussion lists	ftp.nisc.sri.com	(192.33.33.22)
Online Book Initiative (/obi)	ftp.std.com	(192.74.137.7)

Locating Files: archie

- ◆ Indexes nearly all anonymous FTP servers
- ◆ Available at several sites
- ◆ Is automatically updated
- ◆ Searches your pattern in pathname
  - ✓ Search statement: prog word/pattern
  - ✓ archie displays results
  - ✓ Will email results with "mail" command
    example: mail mensch@library.metro.org

archie's Four Search Modes

- ◆ exact — searches for exact match
- ◆ subcase — right and left truncation
- ◆ sub — ignores upper/lower case, and includes R & L truncation
- ◆ regex — = "regular expression" User controls truncation and wildcards

Summary

- ◆ FTP is a service of TCP/IP
- ◆ Over 1500 anonymous FTP sites
- ◆ FTP transfers files between Internet-connected computers
- ◆ Downloading to desktop computer sometimes necessary
- ◆ Locating files simplified by archie

Internet File Transfer Protocol

Internet File Transfer Protocol (FTP) establishes a specialized interactive online session between a local Internet-connected computer and a remote one to allow the transfer of files beween the two computers. FTP is an Internet standard that complies with standard Internet protocol suite, Transmission Control Protocol/Internet Protocol (TCP/IP). "FTP" is the name of the UNIX program that runs the TCP/IP File Transfer Protocol. The command to use this program is the lower-case "`ftp`".

FTP permits the transfer of both ASCII text files, as well as binary files (programs, compressed files, etc.). It is important to remember that files are transferred between the two computers that are directly connected to the network (via ethernet, SLIP, optical fiber, etc.). Files may need to be downloaded to a desktop machine before they can be used.

Most files are transferred using "anonymous FTP," where a site administrator has established a portion of the host computer that can be accessed anonymously by users on the network. Anonymous FTP means that users do not need an account on the host machine, though their access to files may be restricted to certain areas.

File transfer using FTP can be accomplished through a line-by-line terminal interface, as demonstrated here, as well as through client software running on a directly connected computer.

FTP sites offer any number of resources for transfer. There are numerous full-text resources for books, journals, documents of all types, computer programs, statistical resources, graphical images, sounds, etc.) In fact, transfer of files, typically programs, across the Internet is the single most common usage of the network in terms of the amount of data flowing across it.

─────○─────────○─────

Using Anonymous FTP: The Terminal Interface

To use anonymous FTP, the user's desktop or local host computer must be connected to the Internet. Enter the command:

> ftp <*hostname/hostaddress*>   *e.g.,* `ftp sumex-aim.stanford.edu`

When you are prompted for a login, enter:

> **anonymous**   *e.g.,* `anonymous`

When you are prompted for a password, enter:

> *your e-mail address*   *e.g.,* `user@computer.place.domain`

You should now be connected to the remote computer and can use FTP commands to look at the directories and transfer files (refer to the handout "FTP Commands"). To obtain a list of FTP commands available at a site, enter "**help**" once connected to the remote host.

─────○─────────○─────

FTP Tips

- Read the "README" file, if one exists. It has that name for a reason: it will often tell you important information about the archive site or the files within a subdirectory.

- If your local computer system has a paging facility such as "more" or "less" (this will display large text files one screen at a time), it is not necessary to transfer a file to display it. Simply "pipe" (|) it to the paging facility like this:
    > **get README |more**

over

Internet File Transfer Protocol

- Remember to switch to binary mode by entering "binary" *before* transferring files that require this mode (all executable files, some compressed formats; refer to the handout "FTP Commands" for tips).
- Look for INDEX files in directories that include many files. These flat files can then be retrieved and searched, viewed or printed so you can find out exactly which files you wish to retrieve.

- If you receive the message that a file you tried to transfer does not exist, first check to make sure that you are in the correct directory. Then double check that you are entering the correct filename *and* extension, if one exists. Filenames are almost always *case sensitive*, which means you must match the upper and lowercase characters of the filename exactly.

How to Find the File You Need

Often when you use anonymous FTP, it will be to retrieve a file that you know exists at a particular archive site. Sometimes, however, you may want to find a file that you know exists, or you think exists, but for which you have no information on which archive site has the file. You may want to consider the major network archive sites:

Source for:	Site:	IP Address:
Microcomputer software, etc.	wuarchive.wustl.edu	(128.252.135.4)
Macintosh software, etc.	sumex-aim.stanford.edu	(36.44.0.6)
Library-related files	csuvax1.csu.murdoch.edu.au	(134.115.4.1)
	hydra.uwo.ca	(129.100.2.13)
	ftp.unt.edu	(129.120.1.1)
Computers/information	ftp.cni.org	(192.100.21.1)
	ftp.eff.org	(192.88.144.4)
	educom.edu	(192.52.179.128)
Center for Text & Tech.	ftp.guvax.georgetown.edu	(141.161.1.2)
Supreme Court Rulings	ftp.cwru.edu	(192.22.4.2)
Medical materials	ftp.sura.net	(128.167.254.179)
List of discussion lists	ftp.nisc.sri.com	(192.33.33.22)
Online Book Initiative (/obi)	ftp.std.com	(192.74.137.7)

Or, you may wish to connect to an "archie" site and search the database. Archie is a database comprised of the identities and locations of thousands of programs contained by over 1,000 FTP archive sites around the world. By connecting to archie and searching on a filename or a portion of a filename or directory name, you can locate files that match your search and discover where they are located. To search archie, Telnet to archie.unl.edu or 129.93.1.14 and login as "archie". Enter "help" for more information on searching the database. There are also other archie sites in locations around the world. To locate other sites, telnet to archie.mcgill.ca or 132.206.44.21 and login as "archie". *For more detailed information on archie, see "archie: The Index of FTP Archives."*

FTP Commands

The following list of commands are the tools you need to transfer files to and from Internet–connected computers. Please be aware that, although these commands are specified by network protocol specifications, not all commands are supported at every site.

Basic Commands

ftp *<machine address>*   Establishes an FTP session with the named machine; the machine address may be specified with either the domain name address (e.g., `sumex-aim.stanford.edu`) or the numeric IP address (e.g., `36.44.0.6`)

ls   Lists the files and directories in the current directory

dir   Lists the files and directories in the current directory with an indicator of whether an item is a file or a directory, the owner, the date of last update, and in the case of a file, its size in bytes

cd *<directory name>*   Changes the directory on the remote host to the one named

get *<filename>*   Transfers the remote file specified by "filename" to your local computer; to change the name of the file on your local computer, add the local filename to the end of the command (e.g., `get remotefile localfile`)

binary   Changes the transfer mode from text or ASCII (default setting) to binary (type I); this is required before transferring files of particular types (see section below on file extensions for more information)

ascii   Changes the transfer mode to plain text.(type A)

help   Lists available FTP commands available on the remote host

quit   Disconnects from the remote host and quits FTP

mget *<string>* *   "muliple get" – By using the wildcard character "*" this command transfers all files that match the filename string specified (e.g., the command "`mget *.txt`" would retrieve all files with the extension ".txt") from the remote computer to your local computer

Additional Commands

cdup   Changes the current directory to the "parent" directory or to the one above it (therefore "up" in the heirarchy)

put *<filename>*   Transfers the file specified from your local computer to the remote computer; this operation requires special authorization unless a directory has been created to receive incoming files from anonymous users

mput *<string>* *   "multiple put" – Works like "mget" above only for transferring files from your local computer to the remote computer

lcd *<directory name>*   Changes your current directory on your local computer

---

    David F. W. Robison ©1994

dir <remote_filename> <local_filename> creates a locale file from the directory listing from the remote host

prompt Toggles interactive prompting during mget and mput commands; if interactive prompting is turned on, you will be asked to confirm each file transferred

pwd Prints (displays) the name of the current working directory on the remote machine

bye Synonym for **quit**

remotehelp Requests help from the remote FTP server; if a command name is also specified (e.g., `remotehelp cdup`) it is supplied to the server as well

Common File Extensions

Extension	Transfer Mode	Object Type
.asc	A	ASCII text document
.exe	B	IBM PC executable
.gif	B	GIF file (use GIF viewer or converter)
.gz	B	GNU Compression (use **gunzip filename** to uncompress)
.hqx	A	Encoded with the Macintosh application, BinHex (use BinHex to uncompress)
.mac	B	Macintosh executable
.ps	A	PostScript® document
.rtf	A	Rich Text Format (RTF) (use word processor translator)
.sea	B	Self extracting Macintosh archive (double click to uncompress)
.sit	B	Archive created by Macintosh application, StuffIt (use UnstuffIt to uncompress)
.src	B	Source code
.tar	B	Archive created with UNIX tar command (use **tar - x filename** to uncompress)
.tif	B	TIFF file (a graphics format)
.txt	A	Plain text document
.z	B	GNU Compression (use **gunzip filename** to uncompress)
.Z	B	Compressed with UNIX compress command (use **uncompress filename** to uncompress)
.zip	B	DOS file compressed with PKZIP (use **PKUnzip filename** to decompress)
A = ASCII	*B = binary*	

archie: The Index of FTP Archives

- *Where to use archie (telnet to):*

archie.rutgers.edu	128.6.18.15	Rutgers University
archie.unl.edu	129.93.1.14	University of Nebraska in Lincoln
archie.ans.net	147.225.1.10	ANS archie server
archie.au	139.130.4.6	Australian server
archie.funet.fi	128.214.6.100	European server in Finland
archie.doc.ic.ac.uk	146.169.11.3	UK/Europe server
archie.ac.il	132.65.20.254	Israel server
archie.wide.ad.jp	133.4.3.6	Japanese server
archie.kuis.kyoto-u.ac.jp	130.54.20.1	Japanese server
archie.ncu.edu.tw	140.115.19.24	Taiwanese server
archie.sogang.ac.kr	163.239.1.11	Korean server
archie.nz	130.195.9.4	New Zealand server
archie.th-darmstadt.de	130.83.128.111	German server
archie.luth.se	130.240.18.4	Swedish server

   login as "archie"

Searching archie

- **To search for an item, type:**
  prog <word/string>

  where *<word/string>* is replaced by a word or string from the name of the item being searched.

- **To search against the descriptions of software in the database, type:**
  whatis <word/string>

  where *<word/string>* represents part of the description of the item being searched.

- **To stop a search in progress and view the results, type <ctrl-c>**

- **To erase a line of input, type <ctrl-u>**

- **To e-mail the results of the last search, type:**
  mail <address>

  where *<address>* is the full Internet address of the intended recipient of the results of the search.

- *Setting search parameters:*

set search exact	Searches the text as input, case sensitive, without implicit truncation
set search subcase	Sets the search to be case sensitive, with right and left truncation
set search sub	Sets the search to be case insensitive and right and left truncation

- *Setting other session parameters:*

set autologout <#>	Sets the number of minutes of inactivity before being logged out
set mailto <address>	Sets the address to which archie will automatically mail results
set maxhits <#>	Sets the maximum number of matches before archie will stop searching automatically
set pager	Sets archie to display results a screen at a time
set sortby <term>	Sorts output by specified term, such as hostname, time, size, filename, none; an "r" before the term (i.e. set sortby rsize) will sort the output in reverse order

E. Trainer's Aids

Lesson Plan

Teaching Tips

Lesson Plan

Use this lesson plan to create a class that suits your needs best. It is divided into modules that allow you, as the instructor, to pick and choose according to the time available and sections that need to be covered. Each module has an associated set of presentation slides listed to make it easy to select the appropriate slides. If you proceeded through each module, the entire class would take nearly six hours, including two 20-minute breaks and a lunch hour.

The times listed are only advisory, as different instructors move at different paces, and different classes do too. Don't worry that you'll run out of material. Most often, students will want more time to conduct hands-on work (assuming this is possible in the classroom) and will usually be happy to fill the extra time in this manner. Besides, with a subject like FTP, it is unlikely that the presentation will end too soon.

For the online demos, feel free to use the exercises. Many students will want to see you do it first anyway. Otherwise, in addition to, or instead of the exercieses, you may create demos that are related to the specific subject interests of the students in the class.

Don't skip the debriefing after the hands-on sections where you can discuss common problems. This will give everyone a chance to go over the tricks of FTP'ing live and allow those who might be reticent about asking for help to find out why things might have gone wrong. And remember to add breaks in the class, about 15-20 minutes for each two hours of class.

Modules

Introduction to FTP	(slides 1-17: 30 mins.)
The FTP Sesssion	(slides 18-24: 20 mins.)
Online Demo	(10 mins.)
Hands-On	(exercises 1-3: 20 mins.)
Debrief/Questions	(10 mins.)
Downloading & File Types	(slides 25-31: 30 mins.)
Online Demo	(15 mins.)
Hands-On	(exercise 4: 20 mins.)
Debrief/Questions	(10 mins.)
FTP Client Software	(slides 32-33: 10 mins.)

If clients are available in the classroom:

Online Demo	(10 mins.)
Hands-On	(exercise 4: 10 mins.)
Debrief/Questions	(10 mins.)
Locating Files/Archie	(slides 34-48: 30 mins.)
Online Demo	(10 mins.)
Hands-On	(exercise 5: 20 mins.)

If no GIF viewer is available, **get** `<ftp://ftp.uu.net/usenet/news.answers/Quaker-faq.Z>` *which is com pressed; have the class* **uncompress**, *then read the file using* **cat Quaker-faq**

Debrief/Questions	(10 mins.)
Summary	(slide 49: 10 mins.)

Tips for Trainers

FTP tends to be one of the more difficult subjects for students of the Internet. There are at least a couple of reasons for this. First, the very fact that the operation deals with transferring files of almost any size from one computer to another makes people nervous. This nervousness is compounded by the fact that they are connecting to someone else's computer. The best way to combat this obstacle is to remind students that they can not "break" the computer through normal use and that computer systems are designed to withstand human error. If something does, in fact, break down through normal use, it means there was a deficiency in design and/or implementation.

Another factor that discourages new users, is the rather opaque Unix interface that most people must learn. Here it is helpful to do at least one demonstration for the class, slowly, and with clear expanations. Be sure to show the students the directory listing of the local account both before and after the transfer to help demonstrate that a copy of the file has been added to the local account. Encourage the students to read screen displays carefully since they will help the student follow the transaction as it progresses.

Where's the File?

When using the terminal client by connecting to a local host, many students have trouble understanding where the copy of the file that was transferred resides. It is important to explain that the file is on the local host, not the desktop computer until it is downloaded. It's a good idea to use the term "transfer" for moving files between Internet hosts, and "download" only when discussing the transfer and translation of file from an Internet-connected computer to a non-connected desktop computer.

Using this Text and Teaching a Class

In Section C is a set of presentation slides that can be photocopied onto transparencies or the disk version can be presented live on a Macintosh or DOS computer running MS Windows, using a display panel (monochrome or color) and an overhead projector. The presentation on disk is a Microsoft PowerPoint presentation that can be viewed using the viewer included on the disk. If you have a copy of the original program, you will be able to make changes to or print the presentation. The PowerPoint viewer is free of licensing restrictions, so feel free to make copies of it. The presentation itself, however, carries the copyright of the author of this book. Please see the copyright statement that appears on the page beginning Section C.

Section D is designed to be used by trainers to support classes. The exercises in this section can be used by students in a class as part of the text or photocopied and distributed to students. The set of handouts which follows the exercises should be photocopied by either students or teachers. The handouts are designed to function without the book, offering a handy reference tool.

F. Index

Macintosh, client software for 15-16
Mosaic (client software) 16, 17, 18
MS Windows (DOS), client software for 16-17

Net-Happenings 25
Net-Resources list 25
nftp 18
NSCA Telnet (client software) 16, 17

operating systems, FTP available on 3-4

PPP as means of network connection x, 15
presentation slides 27-56
   in handout 71-75

Rapid Filer (client software) 16
reading a text file without transferring (exercise) 64
remote machine, transferring to 6
resource discovery 19
resources, how to find 19

sample FTP session 9-11
search modes, archie 23
security of files on computers 4
simple FTP interface 5
sites, FTP 19, 20
SLIP as means of network connection x, 15
starting an FTP session 6

TCP/IP ix, 3
   definition of 60
Telnet, definition of 60
text file, reading without transferring (exercise) 64
   transferring (exercise) 63
tips (for instructor) 86-87

trainer, notes to 3, 25
trainer's aids 83-87
transferring
   a font (exercise) 67
   a GIF (graphics) file (exercise) 68
   a program (exercise) 66
   a text file (exercise) 63
   to a remote machine 6
Transmission Control Protocol/Internet Protocol 60
type A, ASCII text mode transfer setting 6
type I, binary mode transfer setting 6

Uniform Resource Locator 15, 19, 60
Uniform Resource Number 60
Unix (client software for) 18
Unix and FTP ix, 3-4
URL 15, 19, 60
URN 60

vanilla FTP interface 5

WAIS 61
whatis (archie command) 24
Wide-Area Information Server 61
Windows (MS Windows), client software for 16-17
World-Wide Web 61
WWW 61

Xmodem 14

Yanoff's list, use to find archive sites
Ymodem 14

Zmodem 14